HORSES

The Appaloosa Horse

by Sarah Maass

Consultant:
Diane Rice
Editor
Appaloosa Journal
Moscow, Idaho

Capstone press

Mankato, Minnesota

Edge Books are published by Capstone Press,
151 Good Counsel Drive, P.O. Box 669, Mankato, Minnesota 56002.
www.capstonepress.com

Library of Congress Cataloging-in-Publication Data
Maass, Sarah.
    The Appaloosa Horse / by Sarah Maass.
    p. cm.—(Edge Books. Horses)
    Summary: "Describes the Appaloosa horse, including its history, physical
features, and uses today"—Provided by publisher.
    Includes bibliographical references and index.
    ISBN 0-7368-4372-8 (hardcover)
    1. Appaloosa horse—Juvenile literature. I. Title. II. Series.
SF293.A7M24 2006
636.1'3—dc22   2004030225

Editorial Credits
Carrie A. Braulick, editor; Juliette Peters, designer; Deirdre Barton, photo
    editor/photo researcher

Photo Credits
Capstone Press/Gary Sundermeyer, 8, 23; Karon Dubke, 14, 27 (top)
Courtesy of Appaloosa Journal Inc., 7, 9, 13, 25; B.K. Miller Photography,
    27 (bottom); J. Branam, 22
The Greenwich Workshop Inc., 5
Jennifer Wardrop, 20
Lynn M. Stone, back cover, 11
Mane Photo, cover
Mark J. Barrett, 12, 16–17, 29
Rita K. Nicholson Photography, 19
Ron and Pam McKenzie, 15

1 2 3 4 5 6 10 09 08 07 06 05

Table of Contents

Chapter 1: Famous War Horses............. 4

Chapter 2: Spotted Performers 10

Chapter 3: Working Cow Horse
            Winners 18

Chapter 4: Appaloosas in Action 24

FEATURES

Photo Diagram 16

Fast Facts.. 28

Glossary 30

Read More 31

Internet Sites.. 31

Index... 32

Famous War Horses

Hundreds of years ago, ancestors of the Appaloosa were favorite horses of American Indians. Indians used the spotted horses to help them hunt animals and fight in battles. Today, Appaloosas are still many people's favorite horses. They are known for their speed and ranching abilities.

Coming to North America

In the early 1600s, Spanish settlers came to North America. They brought horses with them. Some of the horses were spotted.

Learn about:
- ★ First breeding programs
- ★ Chief Joseph Trail Ride
- ★ Modern Appaloosas

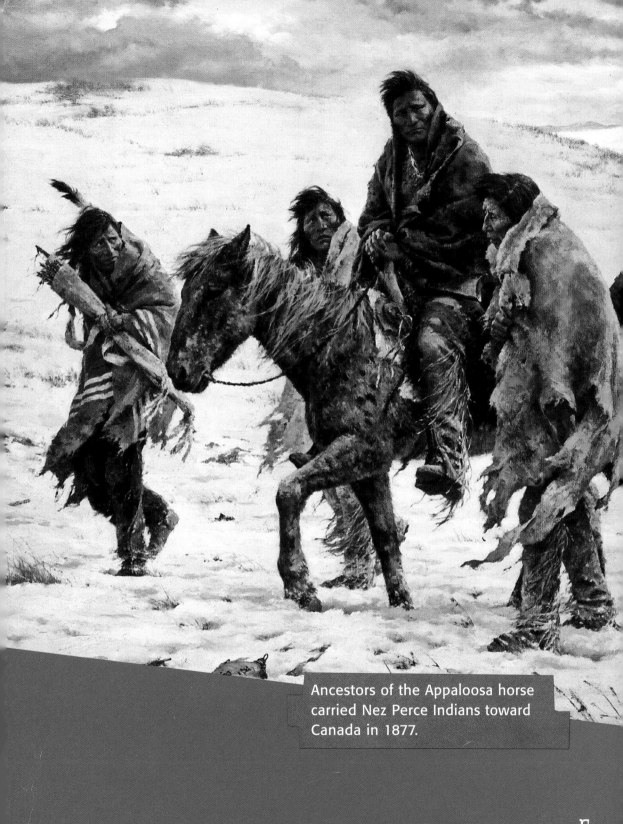

Ancestors of the Appaloosa horse carried Nez Perce Indians toward Canada in 1877.

The Spanish settlers met American Indians who were already living in North America. The settlers and Indians had many disagreements. Soon, they battled against each other. During battles, Indians took some of the settlers' horses.

The Nez Perce

By the early 1700s, the Nez Perce Indians had many horses. The Nez Perce lived in what is now the northwestern United States. They especially liked spotted horses. On these horses, the Nez Perce could easily sneak up on animals they were hunting. The horses' spots blended with the surroundings.

The Nez Perce started breeding programs with their spotted horses. They produced athletic horses that were useful for hunting and in battles.

The Nez Perce War

In 1877, U.S. government leaders wanted to give the Nez Perce's land to settlers. U.S. soldiers attacked the tribe. The attack started the Nez Perce War. Chief Joseph fled with his tribe north toward Canada. The soldiers chased the Nez Perce. The Indians' fast, skillful horses helped them defeat the soldiers in many battles.

After several months, Chief Joseph decided to stop fighting. U.S. soldiers took the Indians' horses. They killed most of the horses and gave the rest to settlers. The settlers called the spotted horses Appaloosas.

Chief Joseph Trail Ride

Each summer, the Appaloosa Horse Club (ApHC) holds the Chief Joseph Trail Ride. The ride covers a 100-mile (161-kilometer) section of the Nez Perce Trail. The trail follows the route of the Nez Perce Indians during the Nez Perce War. The trail begins near Joseph, Oregon, and ends near Chinook, Montana. It covers about 1,300 miles (2,000 kilometers). Hundreds of riders participate in the Chief Joseph Trail Ride each year.

Ranching Horses

In the late 1800s, many settlers in the western United States owned ranches. Large, muscular horses helped ranchers move cattle.

Settlers bred Appaloosas with their large horses. The offspring were more muscular than the horses from the Nez Perce. But the settlers still called these horses Appaloosas. Appaloosas became popular on ranches.

The ApHC

In 1938, Appaloosa owners formed the Appaloosa Horse Club (ApHC). They began registering their horses with the club. The club kept track of each registered horse's ancestry.

Within a few years, many horses were registered with the ApHC. Joker B. and Absarokee Sunset became two of the registry's most important stallions. Many of today's Appaloosas are descendants of these horses. The ApHC now has about 660,000 registered horses.

At first, settlers called the spotted horses from the Nez Perce "Palouse horses." The Palouse River ran through the area where the Nez Perce had lived. Settlers slurred "a Palouse horse" to "Apalousey." Later, the name became Appaloosa.

Joker B. competed in rodeos and other competitive events.

9

Chapter 2

Spotted Performers

Many people recognize Appaloosas by their spotted coat patterns. Appaloosas also are known for their cooperative personalities. The horses seem willing to do their best at any job.

Colors and Coat Patterns

Appaloosas can have one of many coat colors. Many Appaloosas are brown, black, gray, or white. Some Appaloosas are a red-brown color called bay. Bay horses have black manes and tails. They also have black coloring on their lower legs.

Learn about:
★ Coat patterns
★ Mottled skin
★ Scleras

Many Appaloosas have white patches or spots on their rumps.

FACT
Some people call Appaloosas "raindrop horses." The spots on many Appaloosas look like raindrops.

Leopard Appaloosas have white coats covered with dark spots.

The ApHC recognizes many coat patterns. Horses with a blanket coat pattern have a solid white patch on the rump or hip area. Some Appaloosas have a blanket with dark spots in it.

Appaloosas also can have leopard, snowflake, frost, or solid coat patterns. Leopard Appaloosas have white coats with colored spots. Snowflake and frost Appaloosas have dark coats with small white spots or specks. Appaloosas with solid coats have no spots. Solid coat patterns are not as common as spotted ones.

An Appaloosa's white sclera is visible near the corners of the eye.

Breed Features

Many features of Appaloosas help set them apart from other breeds. Appaloosas have mottled skin. Mottled skin is pink. It has a speckled or blotchy pattern of dark spots. Mottled skin often is visible on the nose and around the eyes.

Appaloosas also have white scleras. The sclera surrounds the colored part of the eye. Most other horses have dark scleras.

Many Appaloosas have dark or light stripes on their hooves. These stripes can be wide or narrow.

Body Build and Size

Appaloosas have a mix of breeds in their ancestries. This mix gives each Appaloosa a slightly different body build. To be registered, Appaloosas must have one parent that is an Appaloosa. The other parent can be an Appaloosa, Arabian, Quarter Horse, or Thoroughbred. Foals that have an Arabian parent often are leaner and smaller than foals with a Thoroughbred or Quarter Horse parent.

Overall, Appaloosas have a sturdy look. They have sloped shoulders, strong legs, and tough hooves. Many Appaloosas have muscular hindquarters.

Appaloosas are measured from the ground to the top of their shoulders, or withers. Most Appaloosas are 14.2 to 16 hands tall. A hand equals 4 inches (10 centimeters). Appaloosas usually weigh between 1,000 and 1,200 pounds (450 and 540 kilograms).

Personality

Appaloosas are calm, patient, and cooperative. Their personalities make them good horses for children and new riders. Some stable owners keep Appaloosas as lesson horses. They use the horses to teach students how to ride.

Some children compete with Appaloosas in jumping events.

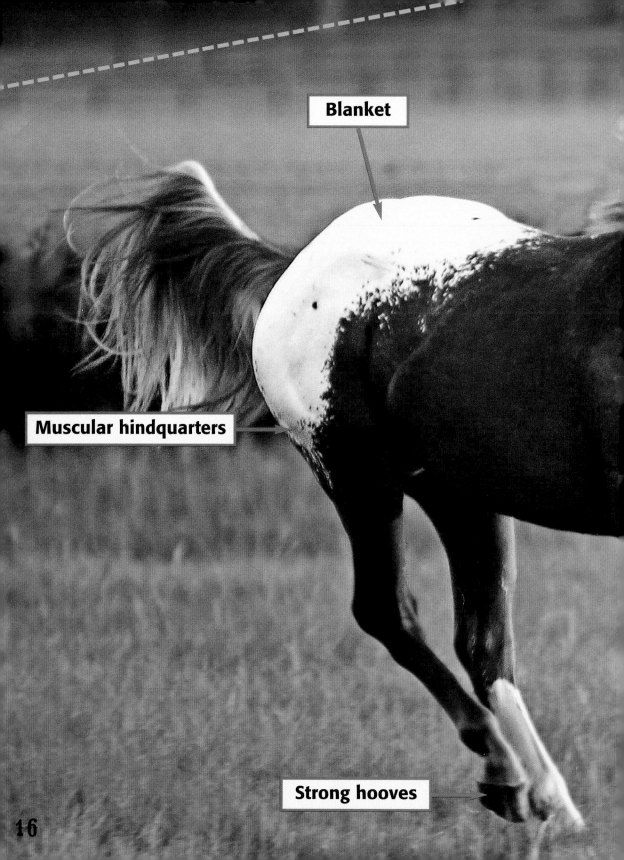

Blanket

Muscular hindquarters

Strong hooves

16

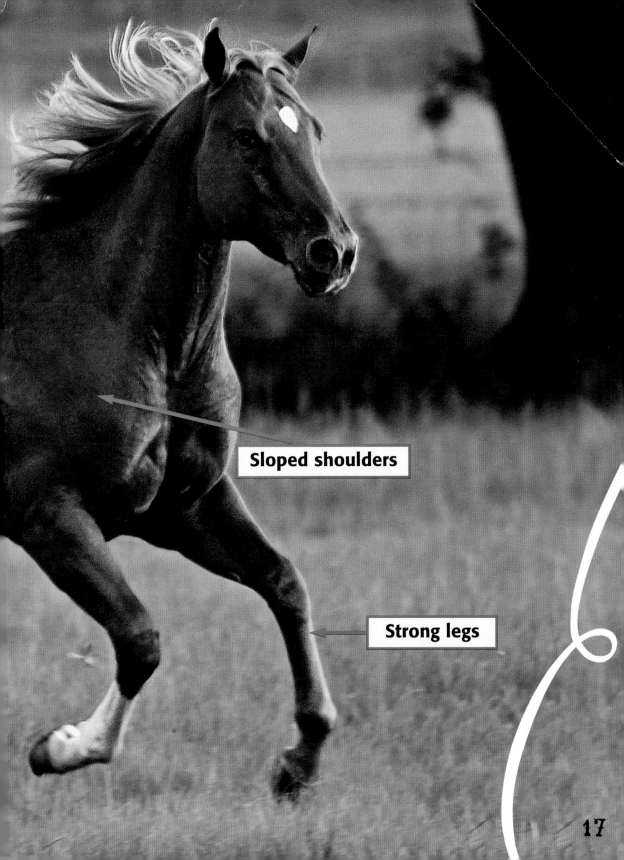

Sloped shoulders

Strong legs

Chapter 3

Working Cow Horse Winners

Appaloosas seem to have a natural ability to herd cattle. People still use Appaloosas on ranches. Some Appaloosa owners show their horses' ranching skills in competitive events.

Working Cow Horse Events

Many Appaloosas do well in working cow horse events. Horses in these events compete in reining, herd work, and fence work.

In reining, the horse and rider do a pattern alone in an arena. They do fast, big circles and slow, small circles. They also perform spins and sliding stops. Reining shows how well the horse and rider work together.

Learn about:
★ **Scoring working cow horse events**
★ **Snaffle bits**
★ **NRCHA events**

A horse's sliding stop often causes dirt to fly in the air.

19

In fence work, riders force a cow to move along a fence.

In herd work, the horse and rider move cows out of a herd. They have 2½ minutes to keep as many as three cows away from the herd. Herd work shows the horse's ability to control cattle.

The horse and rider work with one cow in fence work. At a high-speed gallop, they move the cow along a fence. They make the cow turn around. The horse and rider also move the cow to the middle of the arena.

Judges give participants 60 to 80 points for each part of a working cow horse event. The scores for each part are combined. The rider with the most points wins the event.

Appaloosas must stay focused as they work cattle.

Training

Training a top working cow horse takes several years. Most 2-year-old horses are ready to begin training. Trainers fit the horses with a saddle and a bridle. The bridle holds a metal piece in the horse's mouth. This piece is called a bit.

At first, horses wear a snaffle bit. A snaffle bit is gentle on the horse's mouth. It often has two metal parts that are linked together.

Early in their training, horses learn to stop, start, and turn. Later, they learn how to work cattle and do maneuvers at fast speeds.

Competitions

Appaloosas compete in many working cow horse competitions. The National Reined Cow Horse Association (NRCHA) holds many competitions in the United States. NRCHA events are separated into classes based on the age of the horse and rider.

The most popular NRCHA event is the World Championship Snaffle Bit Futurity. This event is held each year in Reno, Nevada. It is for 3-year-old horses of any breed. About 800 horses compete in the 13-day event. In 1989, Ima Jo's Doll became the first Appaloosa to win the event.

Chapter 4

Appaloosas in Action

Appaloosas do well in activities other than working cow horse. Many Appaloosas separate cows from herds in cutting events. Appaloosa stallion Ima Doc O'Lena has won two ApHC World Championship titles in cutting. In 1996, the ApHC inducted Ima Doc O'Lena into its Hall of Fame.

On the Track

The Nez Perce bred their horses to be fast. Today, Appaloosas speed around racetracks in 10 states. Appaloosas are fastest in races that are .25 to 1 mile (.4 to 1.6 kilometers) long.

Learn about:
★ Appaloosa races
★ Horse show classes
★ Caring for Appaloosas

Appaloosas that race have long, ground-covering strides.

An Appaloosa named Ole Wilson holds the world record for running the fastest time for 4.5 furlongs. This distance is about .5 mile (.8 kilometer). Ole Wilson finished the race in 49.8 seconds.

In the Show Ring

The spots of Appaloosas make them stand out at horse shows. Horse shows include many events called classes. People ride horses in some classes. In halter classes, handlers lead their horses around the ring. Horses are judged on their build and movement.

Each year, about 1,000 horses compete at the ApHC's World Championship Appaloosa Show. The nine-day show has at least 100 classes.

Care

Like all horses, Appaloosas need a great deal of care. Owners must provide their horses with food and water every day. Horses also must have regular grooming, exercise, and hoof care.

Appaloosas attract attention to themselves in any activity they do. The future of the breed looks bright as more people become interested in these talented, flashy horses.

Pay N Go

A leopard Appaloosa named Pay N Go is a well-known dressage horse. At dressage competitions, riders and their horses do a pattern of advanced moves. Judges score the horses and riders based on their performance. Pay N Go competes at the Grand Prix dressage level. Grand Prix is the highest level in dressage. In 2004, the Breyer company made a model horse that looks like Pay N Go.

Fast Facts:
The Appaloosa Horse

History: In the 1700s, the Nez Perce Indians bred spotted horses. The Nez Perce used the horses to hunt buffalo and to fight in battles. In the 1800s, early U.S. settlers bred the spotted horses with heavier, more muscular breeds. This breeding created the Appaloosa.

Height: Appaloosas stand between 14.2 and 16 hands (about 5 feet or 1.5 meters) tall at the withers.

Weight: 1,000 to 1,200 pounds (450 to 540 kilograms)

Features: spotted coats; mottled skin; striped hooves; white scleras; strong legs and hooves; sloped shoulders; muscular hindquarters

Colors: bay, black, brown, white, gray, chestnut, roan

Personality: calm, gentle, cooperative

Abilities: Appaloosas do well in working cow horse events. They also have racing, ranching, and jumping abilities.

Life span: about 25 to 30 years

Glossary

ancestor (AN-sess-tur)—a member of a breed that lived a long time ago

dressage (druh-SAHJ)—a riding style in which horses complete a pattern while doing advanced moves

gait (GATE)—the manner in which a horse moves; gaits include the walk, trot, canter, and gallop.

registry (REH-juh-stree)—an organization that keeps track of the ancestry for horses of a certain breed

sclera (SKLARE-uh)—tough tissue that surrounds the colored part of a horse's eye

snaffle bit (SNAH-fuhl BIT)—a gentle bit used for training young horses; snaffle bits often are made of two metal pieces that are linked together.

stallion (STAL-yuhn)—an adult male horse that can be used for breeding

withers (WITH-urs)—the top of a horse's shoulders

Read More

Barnes, Julia. *101 Facts about Horses and Ponies.* 101 Facts about Pets. Milwaukee: Gareth Stevens, 2002.

Gruber, Beth. *Horse Sense.* Pet's Point of View. Minneapolis: Compass Point Books, 2005.

Ransford, Sandy. *Horse and Pony Breeds.* Kingfisher Riding Club. Boston: Kingfisher, 2003.

Internet Sites

FactHound offers a safe, fun way to find Internet sites related to this book. All of the sites on FactHound have been researched by our staff.

Here's how:

1. Visit *www.facthound.com*
2. Type in this special code **0736843728** for age-appropriate sites. Or enter a search word related to this book for a more general search.
3. Click on the **Fetch It** button.

FactHound will fetch the best sites for you!

Index

American Indians, 4, 6
    Nez Perce, 6–7, 8, 9, 24
Appaloosa Horse Club (ApHC),
    7, 8, 13, 24, 26
appearance, 8, 10, 13, 14
    coat patterns, 13
    colors, 10

battles, 4, 6

care, 26
Chief Joseph, 6, 7
Chief Joseph Trail Ride, 7
cutting, 24

history, 4, 6–8
horse shows, 26
    World Championship
        Appaloosa Show, 26
hunting, 4, 6

Ima Doc O'Lena, 24
Ima Jo's Doll, 23

mottled skin, 13

National Reined Cow Horse
    Association (NRCHA), 23
Nez Perce War, 6–7

Ole Wilson, 26

personality, 15

racing, 24, 26
ranching, 4, 8, 18

scleras, 13
settlers, 4, 6, 7, 8, 9
size, 14
snaffle bits, 23

training, 22–23

working cow horse events, 18, 21,
    23
    fence work, 18, 21
    herd work, 18, 21
    reining, 18
    World Championship Snaffle
        Bit Futurity, 23